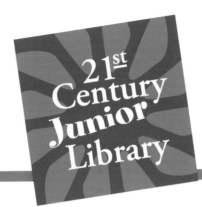

21st Century Junior Library

Katydid

by Michael Shoulders

CHERRY LAKE PUBLISHING * ANN ARBOR, MICHIGAN

Published in the United States of America by Cherry Lake Publishing
Ann Arbor, Michigan
www.cherrylakepublishing.com

Content Adviser: The Entomological Foundation (www.entfdn.org)

Reading Adviser: Marla Conn, ReadAbility, Inc

Photo Credits: © Ryan M. Bolton/Shutterstock Images, cover; © Katarina Christenson/Shutterstock Images, 4; © Dr. Morley Read/Shutterstock Images, 6; © kostin77/Shutterstock Images, 8; © Konstantin Papushin/Flickr Images, 10; © Doug Lemke/Shutterstock Images, 12; © Liew Weng Keong/Shutterstock Images, 14; © Brberrys/Shutterstock Images, 16; © Dr. Morley Read/Shutterstock Images, 18; © Jason S/Shutterstock Images, 20

LIBRARY OF CONGRESS CATALOGING-IN-PUBLICATION DATA
Shoulders, Michael, author.
  Katydid / Michael Shoulders.
      pages cm.—(Creepy crawly critters)
  Includes index.
  ISBN 978-1-63362-592-1 (hardcover)—ISBN 978-1-63362-772-7 (pdf)—ISBN 978-1-63362-682-9 (pbk.)—ISBN 978-1-63362-862-5 (ebook)
  1. Katydids—Juvenile literature. I. Title. II. Series: Creepy crawly critters.

  QL508.T4S56 2015
  595.7'26—dc23   2015001403

Cherry Lake Publishing would like to acknowledge the work of the Partnership for 21st Century Skills.
Please visit www.p21.org for more information.

Printed in the United States of America
Corporate Graphics

CONTENTS

A katydid's antennae are usually
longer than its body.

Grasshopper's Cousin

The katydid is related to the grasshopper and is often mistaken for one. But there is one difference. The katydid's two **antennae** are often longer than its body. Grasshoppers' antennae are usually shorter. The katydid is sometimes called the long-horned grasshopper.

Some katydids have wings that look like leaves.

Some katydids grow to be over 2 inches (5 centimeters) long and are often leaf-green. Their oval-shaped wings have lots of **veins**. The veins resemble those on tree leaves. Katydids hold their wings up over their body. This protects them like a roof shields a house. Katydids also use their wings for **camouflage**, or blending into their environment.

Pink katydids are rare in North America.

Just like people, not all katydids look the same. Many are green, but some are pink. The stripe-faced meadow katydid looks very much like a grasshopper. The leaf katydid blends in perfectly with grass and leaves.

Make a Guess!

Some insects are named after other animals. For instance, zebra butterflies have black-and-white stripes. Can you guess what a peacock katydid looks like? What about a rhinoceros katydid? Or a leaf katydid? Go online with an adult to see if you're right.

Katydids can fly, but they usually climb to where they want to go.

Although they have wings, katydids don't like to fly. They would much rather walk. When they do fly, they usually **flutter** for short distances. A katydid may land on the ground. Then it may walk to a tree or other plant and climb up.

Katydids make loud noises at night in the summer.

Say My Name

Listen closely to the sounds of nearby animals on summer nights. You may hear one that is louder than all the others. Can you hear three quick sounds, followed by four more? That means a katydid is nearby. The male seems to be saying, "Kay-tee-DID. Kay-tee-DIDN'T." This is how the katydid got its name.

Katydids hear sounds through slits in their legs.

Both male and female katydids produce sounds. They rub their front wings together to sing to each other. Some of the sounds katydids produce can't be heard by humans. But they can be heard by other katydids. Katydids do not have ears, however. They hear sounds through special slits on their front legs.

Look!

Look closely at the picture. Can you find the opening in the katydid's leg that picks up sounds?

Many katydids are the same color as the plants where they spend most of their time.

Hide and Go Seek

One way katydids protect themselves is by camouflage. Since they spend most of their time on plants, many look exactly like leaves. Some are brown, while others are green. Some have spots, and others have

Create!

Many katydids camouflage themselves to blend in to their surroundings. Draw and color a katydid. Surround it with shapes that look similar, such as leaves, sticks, and tree bark. Challenge your friends to find your katydid.

This katydid has found something to eat.

slits like torn leaves. They blend in with plant leaves.

Katydids mostly eat leaves, bark, flowers, and seeds. But be careful! Some katydids can bite. Some are **carnivorous**, meaning they eat meat. They will attack and eat grasshoppers, crickets, and small **vertebrates** like lizards.

This katydid is molting.

Life Cycle

Katydids go through three stages of growth. The female lays eggs. Soon the eggs hatch and **nymphs** crawl out. They look like tiny adults without wings. They **molt** several times. Eventually they are adults and grow wings. Adult females also lay eggs. For some katydids, all of this takes a year. Others have even less time to go through their **life cycle**.

GLOSSARY

antennae (an-TEN-ee) thin sensory organs on the heads of insects

camouflage (KAM-uh-flahzh) disguise or natural coloring that allows animals to avoid being seen

carnivorous (kahr-NIV-ur-uhs) having meat as a regular part of the diet

flutter (FLUHT-ur) to wave back and forth rapidly

life cycle (LIFE sye-kuhl) the series of changes each living thing goes through from birth to death

molt (MOHLT) to lose old skin so that new skin can grow

nymphs (NIMFS) a name used for some insects, including katydids, that have not yet become adults

veins (VAYNZ) the stiff, narrow tubes that form the framework of a leaf or an insect's wings

vertebrates (VUR-tuh-brits) animals that have a backbone

FIND OUT MORE

BOOKS

Hovanec, Helene, and Kate Ritchey. *Weird Fact Puzzles: Insects*. New York: Sterling Publishing Co, 2009.

Mertz, Leslie. *Extreme Bugs*. New York: Collins: 2007.

WEB SITES

Audubon Nature Institute: Audubon Animals—Pink Katydid

www.auduboninstitute.org/animals /insects-and-their-relatives/ pink-katydid-16369
Learn about the rare pink katydid.

BugFacts.net: Katydid

www.bugfacts.net/katydid.php
Read some basic facts about katydids.

Cincinnati Zoo: Green Leaf Katydid

http://cincinnatizoo.org/blog/ animals/green-leaf-katydid-2/
Read about the green leaf katydid and download a katydid ringtone.

INDEX

ABOUT THE AUTHOR

Michael Shoulders is a retired educator. When not writing, he travels the United States and Europe speaking to children at schools about the "magic of reading." He is a sought-after speaker at schools, for teacher in-service trainings, and at reading conferences.